KARA,
THE
LONELY
FALCON

KARA, THE LONELY FALCON

FATHER
JOSEPH F. GIRZONE

COLLIER BOOKS
Macmillan Publishing Company/New York
Maxwell Macmillan International
New York   Oxford   Singapore   Sydney

Collier Books
Macmillan Publishing Company
866 Third Avenue
New York, NY 10022

Library of Congress Cataloging-in-Publication Data
Girzone, Joseph F.
Kara, the lonely falcon / Joseph F. Girzone. —
1st Collier Books ed.
p. cm.
ISBN 0-02-019903-1
1. Falcons—Fiction. I. Title.
PS3557.I77K37 1990
813'.54—dc20 90-48129 CIP

FIRST COLLIER BOOKS EDITION

10 9 8 7 6 5 4 3

Printed in the United States of America

*Dedicated to every child
of this universe
who truly hungers for peace.*

KARA,
THE
LONELY
FALCON

CHAPTER 1

Ordinarily, birds do not have names nor do they talk as humans talk, but the following story recounts a series of events so strange that, in order to adequately describe the beautiful tale as it unfolded in the life of a very unusual bird, we must give him a name, and also try, in our inadequate manner, to describe and interpret the thoughts and feelings of this creature who, perhaps, is more noble than many beings who are called human.

Kara was a falcon, sleek and strong and beautiful. He had talons as sharp as miniscule, curved daggers and muscles so powerful he could tear apart an animal twice his size. His beak was delicately, cruelly curved to gouge and tear and mutilate. Kara knew his strength and was aware that he was built stronger and sleeker than all the other falcons he had ever seen. His eyes were as keen as two tiny telescopes, set under a terrifying brow that made him look cruel and ruthless. He could fly far up into the sky and soar in the wind, and with his powerful eyes, scan a field and spot a tiny animal running through the grass.

Falcons are known for their power and sharp vision and ferocious ability to kill. They have a beautiful shape constructed for efficiency in speed and power in attack. They are by instinct killers, everything in their anatomy designed for the hunt. But that is the way falcons were created. They don't kill senselessly, only when they are hungry and need food. They attack only what they need to survive. They are not by nature cruel or mean, but they do function with deadly accuracy.

One day, Kara was soaring in a wind current far above the earth. Beneath him, flying gracefully over the tree tops, was a little white dove. Kara was hungry. He hadn't eaten, it seemed,

for ages and this would be his first meal for the day. He carefully computed the dove's speed and distance and took careful aim at the unsuspecting bird, and then shot like a missile from out of the sky, down through space, at incalculable speed. As the little dove flew gently along, Kara's appetite and excitement grew. But, then, a strange thing happened. Kara spotted in a crag on the side of a cliff, where the dove was flying, a nest with tiny doves, cooing happily at their mother's return. Its mate had spotted the falcon plummeting downward, and was frantically trying to warn its lover by flying up and down and making strange sounds, but all to no avail. Down flew the falcon.

Something happened inside of Kara, which made him all at once lose his desire to kill the dove. He saw that this dove was bringing food to the nest and, for the first time in his young life, he felt a strange sadness, which he could not understand. He felt a feeling of guilt, which he had never experienced before. He saw himself about to attack and tear apart this little dove and could feel the anguish of its mate and the helplessness of the baby doves.

With all his power, his sleek beauty and majestic gracefulness, he felt small and unworthy of his greatness. So, just as he was about to sink his daggerlike talons into the dove, he tilted his wings and glided upward to a perch on a branch of a tall, dead tree and watched the dove come to rest on the edge of her nest, her wide-mouthed babies hungrily taking the food from her beak. They were all so happy; the mystified mate still watching the falcon, confused at the strange behavior of this unusual bird.

Kara looked back sadly from his perch, his head tilted to the side, himself confused at his strange behavior. He was terribly hungry, and miserable besides. You would think he would feel proud of himself that he spared the life of that little bird. But how could he feel proud, at not doing what he was made to do for survival?

Still hungry, Kara raised his head and looked over the tree tops into the distance and spotted another falcon coasting lazily, in search of his morning meal. He no longer had the heart to kill. "But I have to kill in order to live," he answered to himself. "How can a falcon exist if he doesn't hunt for his own food? No one will feed me. Maybe if I look for animals who can defend themselves and have an equal chance, then I won't feel guilty. That's what I will do." So, still feeling miserable and more hungry than ever, Kara lifted himself from his perch and with a few powerful flaps of his wings, rose above the tree tops.

How beautiful the sky was, so blue and so vast and so fresh, away up here above the tree tops. He had never noticed things like this before. What was happening to him? Was he going crazy, was he becoming old? All his time before was spent in search of food and what he could find for himself. Now he had these odd feelings of pity for simple, helpless birds he used to tear apart without a qualm. He noticed that the sky was blue and cool and refreshing and beautiful. Did other falcons feel these things or was he becoming strange?

As these new self-conscious thoughts passed through Kara's mind, he noticed a young fox below through the trees. It was not a fully grown fox, but old enough to go off on its own. It was probably, right now, searching for a rabbit or some other small animal for its own breakfast. Should he dare attack an animal as big as this? A falcon never attacked a fox before. They are too sly and too fast and far too dangerous. Unless the fox was caught completely unawares, and unless the first thrust stunned the animal, the falcon would have no chance to escape. Trapped on the ground with no time to spread its huge unwieldy wings, the bird would be destroyed without even a fight.

But, Kara knew he had no choice. At least, the fox had a chance, perhaps a better chance than he. And he wouldn't feel guilty. So he made his decision. Attack. He flew higher into the air for greater speed and force on impact, one hundred, two hundred, three hundred feet higher, ever watching the sly fox below, slinking through the trees. Finally, the fox entered a little clearing, not much of a clearing, but just wide enough to provide unobstructed flight through the air so nothing could slow its dive upon its prey.

Kara took aim and, with all the power of his huge wings, propelled himself to earth at a speed never needed before. Even the wind whistled past the bird's senses. It was thrilling

and dramatic, but for the first time Kara was frightened. No other prey ever had a chance to fight back before. If this fox should ever turn his head and spot him coming, there would be no hope. Down the falcon plunged, at ever-increasing speed, only two hundred feet now, just two brief seconds and then combat. The bird struck, its talons plunged through fur, ripping into the fox's neck. By instinct, the fox twisted his head and Kara shot his needlelike beak into the fox's eye. The fox rolled over on its back in pain, bewildered and stunned. One of the talons had struck a nerve and paralyzed the fox's right leg. The fox tried to reach the bird with its sharp teeth and pull it off its back. But to no avail. It whipped its head against the ground hoping to shake the bird loose, but it was too stunned. The bird kept attacking with its beak, cutting deep into the fox's ear, causing intense pain. The fox tried to stand up and run away, but it had no power. He could not move and was almost blind.

Suddenly, the fox jerked his head to the right and caught the top of the falcon's wing. The bird, afraid its wing might break, let loose of the fox's neck. The fox released it grip for a brief second and the bird fell to the ground, its wing bleeding. Kara bounced backwards away from the fox, as the injured fox tried to move. It made a thrust with its sharp teeth for the bird, but Kara plunged his beak into the fox's nose, causing the animal to shriek in pain.

The wounded fox, realizing he was no match for this shrewd and powerful bird, turned and tried to escape. But Kara was determined. He attacked again and again until the fox lay paralyzed on the ground, blood trickling from its wounds on the dry, dead leaves.

Kara was exhausted. He had attempted something that no other falcon had ever dared before and survived. It was an act of bravery. It was unnatural for a bird to act above his nature, another example of Kara's strange, new behavior. He devoured his meal but still could not shake feelings of guilt at having destroyed another living thing. It didn't help that this fox was about to kill another animal for its food, or that the fox had a chance to defend itself. He still felt the pangs of guilt.

When he finished eating, Kara flew up on a perch to clean his talons and beak and digest his meal. A few little birds flew near and just as fast flew away when they saw the frightening form of the falcon watching them. Kara sat there alone for a long time with his thoughts. He realized for the first time how alone he was and how lonely. Falcons are lonely birds. They have no friends, not even other falcons. Everyone fears them. Even when they fly, they fly not in flocks, but alone, far up into the heavens, gliding, soaring, searching, hungry, and always alone.

As he sat perched high up on the tree top, basking in the warmth of the golden sunshine, he looked like a threatening giant of a bird, silhouetted against the soft blue sky. But, as powerful and as fearful as he looked, there was a sadness inside that made all the world seem empty and his life without purpose or meaning. He knew he could no longer live the way he had lived before. Proudly surveying the vast expanse spread beneath his perch, Kara concluded he could never again kill, even to survive. It was a momentous decision that would radically alter his whole future, a future he knew could be, at best, uncertain and frightening, yet a future that had no other alternatives. He would just have to trust to fate or whatever it was that controlled the destiny of falcons' lives.

He didn't know how long he had been thinking about these things, but he suddenly felt himself hungry again and immediately thought of the fox's carcass. He swooped back down through the trees and eyed the dead animal lying where he had left it, surrounded by a few crows and other birds tearing away at the remains. When they spotted the falcon, they unanimously let out a chorus of strange cries and flew off. But when Kara landed, there was little left to pick. He ate what there was and flew off into the twilight to find a roost for the night.

Kara slept fitfully that night, waking up intermittently, thinking of the strange experiences of the day before, vaguely fearing the tomorrow.

CHAPTER 2

The next morning, the sun rose orange and gold in the vast blue horizon, with feathery clouds sailing like clipper ships across the sky. It was a beautiful day, a dreamy day, a day for a falcon to just soar through the gentle breezes of the crisp morning air.

Kara woke up early and was sad. As beautiful a day as it was, he was not happy. He was afraid. He saw other birds flying in search of their breakfast. He could not. He had made a commitment to himself and no matter what the cost, he would abide by the decision. He would never again kill for food.

But what would he eat? He had seen deer eating grass and leaves and berries. He had seen other birds eating berries. But, they were only small, weak songbirds. Could he exist and maintain his strength on food like that? He watched the little birds searching for food and sheepishly followed them. But, as they saw him coming, they flew away. He felt bad. He wished he could tell them not to be afraid of him. He wanted to be their friend. He flew into the woods and looked around for berry patches, and soon spotted a large patch filled with large succulent raspberries. He landed on top of the bushes, but they collapsed under the weight and he fell through the thorny stems to the ground. He struggled to get loose, and finally freed himself. But how do you get those berries? Little birds just land on top and eat the berries. But he could not do that. He devised a plan. With his beak, he grabbed a large shoot with a great cluster of berries on top, and with his talons stuck firmly in the ground, he shook the stem until the berries fell on the ground. One by one, he ate them. They were strange. The sweet taste surprised him. He had never eaten anything like this before. He shook loose another cluster, and another, until he had eaten his fill. Then he flew up into the trees and looked around. There was a group of animals watching him from a distance, a rabbit, two little squirrels, a few sparrows, and a blue jay. They had never seen such an extraordinary thing, a falcon eating berries in a berry patch. The proud blue jay suspected the falcon was a weakling or a coward and he flew up into the trees toward to falcon to test him. He flew above the falcon and then dove down to jab him with his beak, to see if he would react. As the blue jay approached, the falcon's instinct to attack suddenly flared up, and with a lightning strike of his beak, he grabbed the blue jay. The dumbfounded bird shrieked and desperately flapped his wings to loosen himself from the falcon's viselike grip. Kara wanted more than anything to "finish the job," but, remembering his resolution, he let the frightened bird go free. The bird dropped to the ground, stunned, unable to get hold of himself. He had misjudged the falcon. He was not a weak cowardly bird, but a swift and powerful and cunning bird of prey. But why was he acting so strangely? Why wasn't he out like other falcons on this beautiful morning, looking for animals to kill? Why would he be eating berries? Finally managing to compose himself, the blue jay flew back to the other animals and they began to chatter together in a strange incomprehensible babble.

They all looked at the extraordinary bird and did not know what to make of him, a bird so powerful and so conscious of his strength and yet a bird so foolish, so different, so alone, so set apart from all the others of his kind. Where did he come from? Who was he? What was there about this bird that made him so mysterious, perched so tense and stark against the morning sky? As the little animals began to leave, each filled with wonder about the big bird, Kara rose from the tree and flew up into the clean, fresh summer air.

Lonely and a little sad, he glided gracefully through the air. He looked around at the beautiful blue and gold sky and felt clean and free. It was so much fun, just flying high into the sky and not having to be continually searching, and searching for food. It was the first day of his life that he had not destroyed another

life, and he felt so good and so happy and so wonderfully free, liberated from what had been a necessity of his whole previous existence. But, now, what would he do with his life?

Kara soared and soared to his complete joy and content. He looked up into the sun and rose up higher and higher above the earth and scanned the great world beneath him. At a mile and a quarter higher, he could see a tiny rabbit hopping across a field. He saw a young deer drinking water from a brook trickling down the side of a hill. A herd of cows in a field looked like a herd of ants grazing in a miniature field. Farther down along the tree tops, he spotted a falcon circling around a clearing. A highway cut a path through a woods and across the side of a rocky hillside. It looked like a toy car racing set, fully landscaped in perfectly scaled miniature.

But soon Kara became tired. His strength began to fail him and his powerful wings no longer wanted to fly. He rested and just floated on the air currents as they carried him along in the gentle breeze. He saw rivers and hills

and streams and animals of every sort. He saw
people and wondered what they must be like.
He liked this new strange world of feeling and
thought, but wondered if it was all just a
dream.

CHAPTER 3

The sun was now high in the sky and Kara was very tired. He saw a tree growing out of a rocky crag overlooking the valley. Gliding down, he landed on the perch, wrapped his talons around the branch, looked around listlessly for a few moments, and then fell sound asleep.

He had never fallen asleep before in broad daylight, but then he had never eaten such a breakfast before, nor flown so high and so far.

When Kara awoke, he was surprised to find himself in such an unfamiliar place. He had flown miles from where he had eaten his breakfast. And even though he had no family, he felt lonely away from all the familiar tree tops and hills and fields and all the same animals he was accustomed to seeing each day. But now he was too hungry to fly home. And he was weak. Berries don't give you much strength. Kara needed to find something to eat. He spotted a little chicken in a barnyard not too far away and felt an urge to swoop down and seize it. It would be so easy, and he was so hungry.

He looked around from his perch, but saw nothing. He lifted himself from the tree and glided down through the woods, hoping to spot something. A little rabbit scurried through a thicket. A pheasant was walking through a row of cornstalks. An idea struck him. Pheasants are beautiful birds and they eat corn. Maybe it's not too bad. So Kara flew down into the corn field and tore off an ear of corn and began to peck away. Soon he finished a whole ear and started another. It certainly couldn't compare to rabbit meat or even quail, but if pheasants eat it, maybe he could eat it, too.

The pheasant stood at a distance, watching

cautiously at the strange sight, a falcon eating corn. What an unusual bird! Whoever heard of a falcon eating corn? Kara had come a long way in two days. But how long could he continue to live this way, a way so far removed from his natural instincts?

It was midafternoon, filled with all kinds of sounds. A warm, gentle breeze played a lonely melody as it floated like a warm breath through the corn field. A crow cawing lazily in the distance added another melancholy note to the symphony of sadness Kara could hear all around him.

Near the corn field was a brook playing its own music as it trickled over the rocks creating miniature waterfalls. Kara walked across the few yards to the stream and quenched his thirst in the cool, fresh water, then lifted himself from the ground and flew up into the sky.

He had no difficulty finding his way back "home," which wasn't really home but just the familiar sights he was so accustomed to and where he felt safe. It wasn't even as if he had friends there (falcons have no friends). You have to care for others to have friends. You have to be able to love. Falcons can't love.

They are calculating and ruthless, so everyone fears them. But Kara felt at home among all the familiar trees and animals, even though he meant nothing to any of them.

Kara flew just above the tree line, on course like an arrow, for his own familiar territory. It was as if his course was plotted and programmed by an innate computer, guiding him unmistakably wherever he chose.

All of nature seemed so beautiful, like a giant painted landscape sprung into life with its colors and sounds and motions and creatures of every sort. Strange he had never noticed all these things before, when there it was continually spread out before him every moment of his life, so obvious and so real, yet as if it never really existed. How could he be so oblivious and unaware of something that was so thrilling and so beautiful? He was just beginning to enjoy the thrill of really living and it was an experience filled with such endless fascination and wonderment that he couldn't believe it was real: It seemed more like a trick of the mind that made what once was still life into real life. It was so much fun. All the rest of his life was so dead and colorless that this new life seemed more real as a dream than as something that was really taking place.

But whether it was real or whether it was a dream didn't matter to Kara. He was happy. Although he was still alone and was now conscious of his aloneness, he was happy, and life had for the first time a real meaning, a purpose. He found a joy in trying to be different than he was, better, more perfect, rising above what seemed to be the limits of his birdlike nature with its instincts, its fears, its urges, its appetites. It made him feel proud that he was no longer enslaved to the things that made him a mere bird, but by discipline had broken through the chains of these restrictive limitations to his full potential and, for the first time, made him feel alive.

As he flew along the tree tops and over the stream cutting through the forest, he could see a young deer lapping up water from the stream, and wondered what the life of a deer must be like. Farther up, he noticed a herd of cows grazing in a pasture and wondered what they did all day long. How dull and meaningless their lives seemed to be! A dog was barking as he chased some straying sheep, and

Kara wondered if the dog knew what he was doing and did he enjoy his life.

Finally he was "home" and saw all the familiar sights. Up on the crag of the little cliff, he saw the dove's nest. The little doves were happy. One bird was missing. He looked around and, in the distance, with his keen vision he spotted the dove flying toward the nest; but far above it, sweeping down at lightning speed, was a falcon. The dove would have no chance at all. Kara was confused. He had strange feelings, this time not to attack the dove but to protect it from its attacker. Without analyzing the situation, Kara flew toward the dove, until the dove spotted Kara. Confused, it changed its course and headed for cover under the trees. The attacking falcon had lost its aim and turned in the direction of the dove. Kara followed until the two falcons met just a few feet from the dove hiding on the branch of a tree, barely conspicuous except for his pure white form among the green leaves. The falcon resented the intrusion of Kara. Kara was annoyed that this strange falcon should break all rules of territorial rights and invade his dominion. Kara attacked, more

to protect the dove than to preserve a hunting right he had already relinquished.

The intruding falcon was clearly outmatched and had no choice but to retreat. Without wasting any time, he cleared a fast path through the trees, not even looking back to see if the angry falcon was following.

The dove was bewildered. It had recognized this strange bird that had once spared its life and now a second time had saved it from another certain death. Kara landed on the same perch where the dove sat quivering, But now the dove was not afraid. It looked at Kara and Kara nudged closer to the dove. The two just looked at each other, but said nothing. A bond had just been created between these two birds that once were natural enemies, one the perennial victim, the other the eternal hunter.

Kara raised himself from the branch and flew up over the trees. It was now quiet and peaceful again. He could see the dove flying off to its nest, a striking figure in marble white against the deep green foliage of the trees.

It was late in the afternoon. There were long shadows along the countryside. The cows were moving slowly towards the barns in each of the farms along the route. The echo of little children's playful voices could be heard floating high up in the sky. Kara felt so close to everything. He felt it all belonged to him, the sounds, the animals, the people, everything. He felt wonderfully happy and so peaceful.

The long day was almost closing, like a new episode in a strange tale, and Kara looked around for a place to spend the night. He saw to the right, up near a crag on the hilltop, a tough old juniper bush growing out from a ledge over the cliff. He flew toward it and waited for the sun to go down, then relaxed his muscles and his powerful talons tightly gripped the branch. Soon he was sound asleep.

Kara was too tired to even dream that night. He slept a deep sleep in total oblivion, as if anesthetized by the exhilarating experiences of that beautiful day.

CHAPTER 4

The sun rose like a red hot cherry over the tree tops. The sky was filled with orange and yellow feathers floating across the delicate blue ocean. The air was cool away up on the rocky crag that scanned the vast plain beneath. Kara was already awake, eager to see what adventure the new day would bring. He stretched his huge powerful wings and yawned, or whatever birds do that is equivalent. Life was so beautiful; still, he wished he didn't have to waste time eating, but he was so hungry, he had to eat. He walked along the crooked horizontal tree trunk toward the ledge, which was quite large, a natural home where Kara could feel safe from any possible danger. Now that he no longer was a hunter, other preying birds might think he was a coward and try to attack him. Here he would be safe, far above where most birds of prey feel comfortable.

The early morning is the most beautiful time of the day. Kara was eager to fly, and was anxious to get over his breakfast so he could go out and discover new adventures. Rather than spend unnecessary time looking for different food, Kara decided to eat at the same places as the day before. So, with his computerized directional system, he immediately located the berry patch where he met the little animals who were so shocked at his behavior. He floated down and rested on a large stalk and began to pick the berries. They tasted a little better than the day before. He kept picking and eating. The noise his huge body made in the berry patch attracted attention and the familiar little animals began to gather again; the rabbit, the squirrel, the birds, and this time the little white dove, cooing excitedly as if trying to tell the story of the day before. It was odd that no one felt afraid or uncomfortable with Kara. They obviously didn't have the same warm feeling the dove had for the falcon; they were more curious than anything else and, perhaps, were unafraid because of the dove's enthusiastic storytelling. For some vague reason, they also felt much safer in their little corner of the farther woods than they had ever been before. They all seemed to sense they had a protector, if not yet a real friend. So they all watched curiously, even daring to approach the berry patch where Kara was feeding.

He noticed them coming toward him and looked up, by instinct tensely, and just looked at them with his fierce frightening eyes. The little animals started to become frightened, but the little dove reassured them when he flew up on the stalk next to Kara, picked a berry in his little beak and turned toward Kara, ostensibly offering it to him. Kara was deeply touched. No one had ever done anything for him in his whole life, except his mother when he was a little baby. But this beautiful little kindness and token of friendship on the part of a dove was so moving that this powerful bird was overwhelmed with tender feelings for this helpless lovable bird.

He took the berry as delicately as his strong awkward beak permitted and stood there motionless just staring intently at the dove. The little dove spread its wings and flew back down to the other animals who were quite astonished at this strange happening. But they all felt it was beautiful and very touching, and deep down they sort of envied the dove's closeness to that big, powerful bird.

But this little gesture on the part of the dove, as simple as it appeared, evidenced a change inside that bird. Animals, birds included, just don't share with anyone, even their own kind, and here was a weak, gentle dove offering a bit of food to a powerful falcon. The whole event was real cause for wonder as they realized that their outlook toward each other had changed. They had to admit, it was beautiful, the way they now felt toward each other.

This incident was just the beginning of a whole new relationship among all these little animals. Kara still disappeared each day far up into the sky, almost into the heavens, so far up, the animals were concerned. They

watched, in awe, his climbing higher and higher and then soaring, sometimes gliding out of sight far over the distant hills. They missed him when he went because they somehow felt a little bit safer when he was around. The nervous, ornery, little squirrel never wanted to admit it, but he too missed the big bird and didn't feel as safe when he was away.

On one occasion, it was late in the afternoon, as Kara was returning "home," a strange, big bird had chanced to come into their corner of the woods and had spotted the little animals. Their group had grown now. There were at least thirty or forty animals, even new ones; two fat woodchucks, some cardinals, a few chickadees, two robins, a handful of sparrows, a little pheasant family that wandered in from the nearby field, and a small group of quail, a brown squirrel, a skunk whom everyone was at first afraid of, and a tiny deer that wandered away from its mother every now and then, and interesting enough, a young falcon who was trying to imitate Kara.

This one day, a hawk of rather unusual description, though it was almost the size of Kara, happened to wander in upon the group and took them all by surprise. Little rabbits are always fair game, so the bird pounced upon one of the rabbits and sank its powerful daggerlike talons into the helpless rabbit's neck. The rabbit tried desperately and uselessly to free itself, but to no avail. The other animals were horrified but helpless in this sudden attack. The birds tried to fly around the hawk to distract it and make it let go of the little rabbit, but they were beaten off by the bird's powerful wings. But these diversionary tactics served one purpose, to stall the hawk's flying away. This was fortunate because Kara was just returning home from his day's adventure and had spotted from almost a mile away the drama taking place in his "home." He picked up speed and, desperately trying to reach the scene in time, managed to travel at a speed he never attained before, well over one hundred and sixty miles an hour. He was high in the sky and just above the opening in the woods. The cardinals and blue jays were still angrily besieging the confused hawk, who still had the rabbit firmly in his grip. Kara tipped his wings and tail and fiercely flapped his wings, even in his dive. He was traveling close to two hundred miles an hour, down like a bolt of angry black lightning falling from the skies. In an instant, he was upon the bewildered hawk, striking his back and wings with his talons as he swooped past, causing the hawk to drop the frightened rabbit. The hawk was in a rage. He looked up at Kara and refused to leave. Kara came back down and struck again at the hawk. This time, the hawk, jumping off the ground, tried to claw at Kara. Birds of prey are helpless on the ground. Speed in diving and their powerful talons and sharp beaks are their greatest weapons. These two birds were both at a disadvantage, but their anger increased their ferocity. They struck each other with their beaks and clawed with their talons. Kara could have broken the hawk's neck as he plummeted down upon him. But he could no longer kill. So now the duel.

The other animals stood around, some from their perches in the trees, some on the ground, watching the whole drama, the outcome of which would affect their whole future as a new "family." The hawk was angry and vicious, but Kara was calm, conscious of his power, his sharp mind giving him a clear advantage over the dullwitted, clumsy hawk. Finally, Kara raised himself from the ground, seizing the hawk by the throat as he did so, and carried him clear up above the trees. Shocked at the power of this falcon, the hawk thought sure it was the end. High up in the air, Kara dropped the bird who was too numb to fly. He fell some distance before he regained his senses and spread his wings to break the fall. In a moment, he was in control and, in fear, took off, as fast as he could to spread the word about this extraordinary, powerful, but insane falcon who protected all the little animals in the farther woods.

When the hawk was far gone, Kara flew down "home" to assess the fate of the rabbit. Gliding through the trees, he was given a hero's welcome by the whole family as they chanted an unharmonious concert of praise. He had arrived none too soon. A few moments later the hawk would have flown away with his prey. Though the shaken rabbit was bleeding, it would soon heal. All the animals were grateful. They were all subjected to, in varying degrees, possible attack by these powerful

birds, whether they be hawks, falcons, crows, or even blue jays who, surprisingly enough, had not joined their little family.

This incident had shown all the other animals what the dove had been aware of all along, the strange and beautiful nature of the big powerful falcon. Even though he never seemed to be a part of them and lived an existence that seemed so lonely and separated from any warm relationships to any other living thing, there was a kindness and a majesty about Kara that made them love him even if they stood in awe of him. His effect on the lives of all the animals was profound. They helped each other. They even cared for each other when one of them was sick. They had developed, in the course of those months, a whole new way of life, a way of life that brought so much happiness and lighthearted friendships into the petty world of their previous existence, so filled with suspicions and jealousies and fierce competition. And they were none the worse off materially either, because they helped one another and every one benefited. In fact, they were much better off than before and so much happier. Gone was all the fear of each other that made each day so miserable. Now a beautiful peace settled over the whole farther wood because of the presence of this strange, gentle falcon.

CHAPTER 5

Ever since that day when Kara had saved the little rabbit, the animals were very close to Kara, even though they couldn't really consider him one of the family. There was something different about him which made it difficult to become too intimate. But they never doubted his love and care for them and they loved him with a love that bordered on veneration. He was just someone apart, someone really special.

All during the summer and autumn, Kara had no trouble getting food from the fields and woods, but when the harvest was over and the cold months came, there were no berries to be found, no corn in the fields. He watched the other animals to see what they ate during these difficult months. The robins disappeared and were no longer seen. Kara never heard of migration. The squirrels stashed away, in various hiding places throughout the forest, little caches of chestnuts and seeds that helped them survive the winter. The rabbits disappeared into the ground and came out only to make brief forays in search of whatever they could find. Sometimes all they could find was the soft bark on young trees. The woodchucks just disappeared completely into their tunnels in the mound at the edge of the farther wood. The birds ate seeds that had fallen down among the leaves or berries from certain types of bushes.

But Kara could eat none of these things, nor could be hibernate and sleep all winter. He became concerned. Where would he find food for the long, cold winter months. He watched where the farmers brought the corn, and on a few occasions, went to a barnyard to get some corn from the grain bins. But this was too dangerous. The farmers, seeing this great fal-

con, thought he came to steal the chickens and they shot at him with their shotguns. Fortunately, Kara escaped. This was too dangerous. But he still could not solve the problem of where to find food to carry him through the winter.

The little animals seemed to sense his sorry situation and wondered among themselves what they could do to help their friend without letting him know about it. They all decided to "chip in" together and share some of their meager winter rations with Kara. But, knowing that he was proud and independent, they decided to make the trip to the top of the hill, to the crag where Kara spent each night, and quietly leave their gifts in a neat pile on the ledge nearby. This they did for the whole winter, even during the bad, snowy weather. It wasn't much, but it was a beautiful gesture of love and friendship for the kindly falcon who had given them so much by just being there near them and being their friend. He noticed immediately the little pile of seeds and acorns, thoughtfully cracked open, and also some dried grapes and even some tender bark of shrubs. It wasn't much, but it was a lot from the little store each had secured for themselves. The squirrels had to search their memories for places they had hidden nuts during the summer. Squirrels forget most of their hiding places.

Kara knew immediately where all these gifts came from, because he recognized each one's own particular food. But he wondered how they could have been there without his sharp, omniscient senses noticing their presence. No matter, he was grateful for their thoughtfulness, even though he couldn't possibly survive on this small amount of food. He began to eat the tasty breakfast his friends had prepared for him and though he was still quite hungry, he felt he should, in some not too obvious way, show his appreciation to his friends. He lifted himself off the ledge and floated down into the forest, through the trees, to the clearing where all the little animals gathered to share their stories and spread their harmless gossip. They were all there. Kara didn't want to let on he knew what they had done for him, so he had to play ignorant. He merely flew down into the clearing and through the trees, over their heads, just to let them know he was thinking of them. Then he flew on.

He couldn't fly very far that day. He was just too tired and too hungry. Besides, it was cold and it was snowing and there wasn't much point in flying around in the snow. After a short journey across the woods, he decided to go back "home." The afternoon was mostly spent just sheltering himself under the branches of big trees in the woods where he wouldn't be too exposed to the winds blowing through the forest. It was quiet and peaceful in the forest during the wintertime. Everything was beautiful, but in a different way. But it was cold, and lonely.

As the sun began to set, Kara started back up for his crag on the cliff top and began for the first time to think about the sun. It was always so beautiful, even in the winter when it was so cold everywhere. The sun fascinated him. He remembered how much fun it was on warm sunny days to fly high into the sky and feel the warm rays of the sun caressing him as if it possessed him. He felt a strange closeness to the sun and loved just to watch it go to rest at night in a glorious drama of magnificent colors, transforming each moment in a fading panorama of light.

But there was something mysterious about the sun. He felt that everything owed its existence to the sun, and its presence seemed to be everywhere. But when Kara flew high up into the sky to draw closer to the sun, it seemed as if it was still just as far away. For some reason, he loved the sun. He didn't know why, but he felt very safe and warm and peaceful when he was flying up high in the arms of the sun's rays.

These thoughts passed through Kara's mind as he flew up to his rocky retreat for the night. As he reached the ledge, he noticed an unusual plant growing from the cracks in the rocks. It was white, like little mushrooms, but waferlike in shape. Overcome by his hunger, he wondered if he could eat it. He pecked at one timidly and tasted a little. It had a sweet and delicious flavor and was unlike anything he had ever eaten before. He noticed it grew only in one spot, where the last rays of the evening sun fell upon the rocks. He ate more until he almost finished it. He thought of his friends and wanted to save some for them. Perhaps

he could carry some down with him in the morning and share it with them.

As Kara tasted his new food, he noticed it made him feel different inside. Although everything around him was cold and lonely and empty, he felt a warm glow inside. He felt a peace and a joy that he had never known before. He wondered if that food would be there tomorrow night when he came back from his daily flight.

It was now dark and Kara flew out onto the horizontal tree bed and went to sleep, a sleep that was filled with beautiful dreams about the sun and the light and a whole new world where everything seemed made of light, and he slept soundly and happily. He didn't feel alone.

CHAPTER 6

The next day, the sun rose on the other side of farther forest. It was beautiful. Kara felt love for the beautiful sun. He felt he belonged, in some strange way, to the sun, as if he owed his existence to this being whose presence pervaded the whole world. The early morning rays of the sun gently touched Kara each morning as it rose and gave him strength and a feeling of oneness with all the life around him and with what seemed to be the center of life itself, a life which seemed to communicate with him and to share with him ideas and feelings that were not his own.

Now Kara finally realized for the first time the reason and the cause of the vast and powerful transformation within him. It had all been such a mystery, the new inner life he had discovered, the feeling of joy and freedom from all those things that made him just a mere bird of prey, spending each day plotting, calculating, planning, centering everything around the satisfying of his cravings and his needs as a powerful and skilled animal. Now Kara knew that in some way he had been touched by a force, a being, whose existence provided the light and the warmth for all creation, a being who was real, who was alive, who loved him in some beautiful, personal, and intimate way, and was near him every moment. He now sensed that he lived and breathed and even existed in this new presence and he felt ecstatic with a joy and a peace and an exaltation that seemed to lift him outside himself and made him want more than anything else to be one with this source of light and warmth. It was to him not just some thing. It was real, it was alive, it was full of love, like a vast and endless ocean, and even more than that, it was a being who existed, who thought and cared and loved and was close to every living thing, and this being loved Kara and Kara loved him in return and longed to see him, not as reflected in the rays of the sun or in its caressing warmth, but as he is in himself, in all the splendor of his limitless existence.

Kara was so involved in this ecstasy, he forgot everything else. He shook himself and stretched out his huge wings and breathed in the cold morning air. He thought of the food he saved for his friends and turned to look for it. It was gone. He looked over the ledge and the little breakfast cache was lying there waiting. Kara thought, perhaps, his friends may have eaten the new food that he saved for them, but there were no footsteps in the new fallen snow. It just vanished as mysteriously as it came; another strange incident in the life of this strange bird.

He ate the seeds and the acorns and dried grapes and even tried to eat the tender pieces of bark. Though he was still hungry, he was so glad to be alive. The morning was cold, but it was beautiful, with the white snow covering the tree tops and the fields and the whole valley like a soft white blanket. The sun was already up for over half an hour and was bright and warm and radiant, like a beautiful gem in a sea of soft ethereal blue.

Kara glided off the crag and just floated down upon the trees and drifted toward the farther woods. His friends were waiting for him as usual, as he flew through the trees. They just looked and chatted among themseves as he came near and not a word passed between Kara and his friends. Their closeness didn't need words. They all just knew. Sometimes thoughts don't have to be put into words, especially between friends. Thoughts and feelings don't have to be expressed, they are already known and felt. That was the way it was.

As he glided through the clearing, Kara started to climb and flew up high into the morning sky. He traveled far that day and didn't even notice his tiredness or his hunger. As sunset approached, he flew back "home" and as he was about to settle on his perch, he noticed again that strange new food growing right out of the rocks and through the snow, as the last rays of the sun touched that spot.

He ate it until he was filled and only wished he could share this food with his friends.

But it seemed as if there was no way to keep this food for them, because the next morning, it had vanished again. Kara had slept well the night before and had dreams of a place that was so indescridably beautiful that he wished he could be there. This place was like nothing he had ever seen in his whole life. There were sounds and beings he had never heard or seen before. Everything was magnificent, and he had a feeling he was going there and he was happy.

Kara was happier this day than he had ever been before. It was also a beautiful day, and that helped. The sun was more enchanting and thrilling than it had ever been. It seemed like the perfect day. Kara ate his breakfast and flew down to greet his friends. This time, he even talked with them. They were thrilled. They chatted all in their own language and all completely understood. Even the rabbits and the groundhogs were there this morning. Kara stayed with them until almost noon. They shared so many experiences together. Only one "secret" no one talked about, the secret of the sharing of the breakfast. Even Kara didn't mention it because he knew they wanted to keep it a secret.

As noon approached, Kara flew up into the sky. The sun was bright, radiant, more brilliant than anyone had ever seen it. The powerful falcon flew higher and higher into the blue sky. All his friends watched in utter amazement at the power and the grace and beauty of that beautiful being who had become so much a part of their life. As they watched him climb higher into the sun, an awesome occurence unfolded before their eyes. As the golden rays of the sun touched Kara's wings, they seemed to become almost transparent, almost like the sun itself, and his whole form seemed to be transformed and absorbed into the light of the sun's rays. They couldn't believe what was unfolding before their very eyes; perhaps, it was just a mirage, an illusion. They were overcome with a deep sense of sadness which they could not understand.

That day was a long one for Kara's friends. They even waited for him to fly "home" that night. They didn't see him. Perhaps, he came back another way. It was now dark.

The next morning early, they all gathered together to bring their breakfast up to Kara's ledge. They still felt sad and seemed to sense they would never see their gentle friend again.

When they arrived at the ledge, they were deeply saddened, but they were not surprised. Kara was not there. He did not return home. And they knew he would not return home again. But growing out of the rock in the rays of the early morning sun was the wonderful food that Kara wanted so much to share with his friends. They all ate it and were filled with joy. They now understood why that powerful, strange, and gentle falcon was different from anyone they had known before. From then on, each morning they found the mysterious food waiting for them and the lives of all those animals in the farther forest were different from the lives of all the other animals.

And that farther forest is not very far from any one of us.